WITHDRAWN

BY CHARLES WRIGHT

POETRY
The Grave of the Right Hand
Hard Freight
Bloodlines
China Trace
The Southern Cross
Country Music: Selected Early Poems
The Other Side of the River
Zone Journals
Xionia
The World of the Ten Thousand Things: Poems 1980–1990

TRANSLATIONS
The Storm and Other Things (Eugenio Montale)
Orphic Songs (Dino Campana)

NONFICTION
Halflife
Quarter Notes

CHICKAMAUGA

Charles Wright

CHICKAMAUGA

Farrar, Straus and Giroux

New York

Library of Congress Cataloging-in-Publication Data
Wright, Charles
Chickamauga / Charles Wright. — 1st ed.
p.   cm.
I. Title.
PS3573.R52C45   1995   811'.54—dc20   94-45914   CIP
0-374-52481-5

Grateful acknowledgment is made to the following publications, in
whose pages these poems first appeared: The Gettysburg Review, Poetry,
The New Yorker, The New Republic, Antaeus, Field, The Southern
Review, The Amicus Journal, Grand Street, The Wallace Stevens
Journal, The Iron Mountain Review, The Southwest Review, The
Michigan Quarterly Review, The Paris Review, The Colorado Review,
Shenandoah, and The Partisan Review. "Still Life with Stick and Word"
appeared in a book published by The Windhover Press for the
University of Iowa Museum, and "Summer Storm" appeared in
Transforming Vision, published by The Art Institute of Chicago and
Bulfinch Press.

Third printing, 1999

This book is dedicated to

the memory of Howard Moss

of New York City, poet and editor,

who is not forgotten by his friends

Contents

AFTERMATH

Sitting Outside
at the End of Autumn

Three years ago, in the afternoons,
                              I used to sit back here and try
To answer the simple arithmetic of my life,
But never could figure it—
This object and that object
Never contained the landscape
                              nor all of its implications,
This tree and that shrub
Never completely satisfied the sum or quotient
I took from or carried to,
                              nor do they do so now,
Though I'm back here again, looking to calculate,
Looking to see what adds up.

Everything comes from something,
                              only something comes from nothing,
Lao Tzu says, more or less.
Eminently sensible, I say,
Rubbing this tiny snail shell between my thumb and two fingers.
Delicate as an earring,
                              it carries its emptiness like a child
It would be rid of.
I rub it clockwise and counterclockwise, hoping for anything
Resplendent in its vocabulary or disguise—
But one and one make nothing, he adds,
                              endless and everywhere,
The shadow that everything casts.

3]

Lines After
Rereading T. S. Eliot

The orchard is fading out.
                              All nine of the fruit trees
Diminish and dull back in the late Sunday sunlight.

The dead script of vines
                              scrawls unintelligibly
Over the arbor vitae.

A cricket, a little black luck charm,
                              stops at my feet
On his singular pathway

Across the wasteland between the brown
Apricot leaf and the hedge.
                              Hello, good luck, goodbye.

———————

Whatever happened to the dark sublime,
                              sin of the third eye,
Cross-gap between flesh and abstraction?

Pain, the old standby, is what calls us,
A life between the rocks,
                              the desert's sweet syllable.

We cannot forgive ourselves.
When our ears sing our guiltless blood,

                              we cannot forgive ourselves.

We know hell in our bones—
                              outside time, outside comprehension,
We know it in our bones.

                    —————

Ambition is such a small thing.
                              Like a late pear in the autumn sun,
Hard, green, indigestible,

It hangs in front of our eyes.
                              It hangs there and grows dark
As the light of Indian summer seeps away at our backs.

Illustrious and unknown
                              is what we should wish for ourselves,
Fading the way this landscape fades

Into its anonymity
                    and various selves,
So indefinable, so dumb.

Reading Lao Tzu Again
in the New Year

Snub end of a dismal year,
                    deep in the dwarf orchard,
The sky with its undercoat of blackwash and point stars,
I stand in the dark and answer to
My life, this shirt I want to take off,
                    which is on fire . . .

Old year, new year, old song, new song,
                    nothing will change hands
Each time we change heart, each time
Like a hard cloud that has drifted all day through the sky
Toward the night's shrugged shoulder
                    with its epaulet of stars.

————————

Prosodies rise and fall.
                    Structures rise in the mind and fall.
Failure reseeds the old ground.
Does the grass, with its inches in two worlds, love the dirt?
Does the snowflake the raindrop?

I've heard that those who know will never tell us,
                    and heard
That those who tell us will never know.
Words are wrong.
Structures are wrong.
                    Even the questions are compromise.

Desire discriminates and language discriminates:
They form no part of the essence of all things:
                                                 each word
Is a failure, each object
We name and place
                    leads us another step away from the light.

Loss is its own gain.
                      Its secret is emptiness.
Our images lie in the flat pools of their dark selves
Like bodies of water the tide moves.
They move as the tide moves.
                             Its secret is emptiness.

_____

Four days into January,
                        the grass grows tiny, tiny
Under the peach trees.
Wind from the Blue Ridge tumbles the hat
Of daylight farther and farther
                                into the eastern counties.

Sunlight spray on the ash limbs.
                                 Two birds
Whistle at something unseen, one black note and one interval.
We're placed between now and not-now,
                                      held by affection,
Large rock balanced upon a small rock.

Under the Nine Trees
in January

Last night's stars and last night's wind
Are west of the mountains now, and east of the river.
Here, under the branches of the nine trees,
                how small the world seems.

Should we lament, in winter, our shadow's solitude,
Our names spelled out like snowflakes?
Where is it written, *the season's decrease diminishes me?*

Should we long for stillness,
                a hush for the trivial body
Washed in the colors of paradise,
Dirt-colored water-colored match-flame-and-wind-colored?

As one who has never understood the void,
                should I
Give counsel to the darkness, honor the condor's wing?
Should we keep on bowing to
                an inch of this and an inch of that?

The world is a handkerchief.
Today I spread it across my knees.
Tomorrow they'll fold it into my breast pocket,
                white on my dark suit.

After Reading Wang Wei,
I Go Outside to the Full Moon

Back here, old snow like lace cakes,
Candescent and brittle now and then through the tall grass.
Remorse, remorse, the dark drones.

The body's the affliction,
No resting place in the black pews of the winter trees,
No resting place in the clouds.

Mercy upon us, old man,
You in the China dust, I this side of my past life,
Salt in the light of heaven.

Isolate landscape. World's grip.
The absolute, as small as a poker chip, moves off,
Bright moon shining between pines.

Easter 1989

March is the month of slow fire,
                        new grasses stung with rain,
Cold-shouldered, white-lipped.
Druidic crocus circles appear
Overnight, morose in their purple habits,
                        wet cowls
Glistening in the cut sun.

———

Instinct will end us.
The force that measles the peach tree
                        will divest and undo us.
The power that kicks on
                the cells in the lilac bush
Will tumble us down and down.
Under the quince tree, purple cross points, and that's all right

For the time being,
                the willow across the back fence
Menacing in its green caul.
When the full moon comes
                    gunning under the cloud's cassock
Later tonight, the stations
Will start to break forth like stars, their numbers flashing and then some.

Belief is a paltry thing
                 and will betray us, soul's load scotched

Against the invisible:
We are what we've always thought we were—
Peeling the membrane back,
                              amazed, like the jonquil's yellow head
Butting the nothingness—
                    in the wrong place, in the wrong body.

The definer of all things
                    cannot be spoken of.
It is not knowledge or truth.
We get no closer than next-to-it.
Beyond wisdom, beyond denial,
                              it asks us for nothing,
According to Pseudo-Dionysus, which sounds good to me.

                    ————————

Nubbly with enzymes,
The hardwoods gurgle and boil in their leathery sheaths.
Flame flicks the peony's fuse.
Out of the caves of their locked beings,
                              fluorescent shapes
Roll the darkness aside as they rise to enter the real world.

Reading Rorty and Paul Celan
One Morning in Early June

In the skylight it's Sunday,
A little aura between the slats of the Venetian blinds.
Outside the front window,
                         a mockingbird balances
Gingerly on a spruce branch.
At the Munch house across the street,
Rebecca reads through the paper, then stares at her knees
On the front porch.
                   Church bell. Weed-eater's cough and spin.

From here, the color of mountains both is and is not,
Beginning of June,
Haze like a nesting bird in the trees,
The Blue Ridge partial,
                   then not partial,
Between the staff lines of the telephone wires and pine tips
That sizzle like E.T.'s finger.
Mid-nineties, and summer officially still three weeks away.

———————

If truth is made and not found,
                       what an amazing world
We live in, more secret than ever
And beautiful of access.
Goodbye, old exits, goodbye, old entrances, the way
Out is the way in at last,

Two-hearted sorrow of middle age,
                              substanceless blue,
Benevolent anarchy to tan and grow old with.

If sentences constitute
                    everything we believe,
Vocabularies retool
Our inability to measure and get it right,
And languages don't exist.
That's one theory. Here's another:
Something weighs on our shoulders
And settles itself like black light
                         invisibly in our hair . . .

———————

Pool table. Zebra rug.
                    Three chairs in a half circle.
Buck horns and Ca' Paruta.
Gouache of the Clinchfield station in Kingsport, Tennessee.
High tide on the Grand Canal,
                         San Zeno in late spring
Taken by "Ponti" back in the nineteenth century.
I see the unknown photographer
                    under his dark cloth. Magnesium flash.
Silence. I hear what he has to say.

June 3rd, heat like Scotch tape on the skin,
Mountains the color of nothing again,
                              then something through mist.
In Tuscany, on the Sette Ponti, Gròpina dead-ends

Above the plain and the Arno's marauding cities,
Columns eaten by darkness,
Cathedral unsentenced and plugged in
To what's-not-there,

windows of alabaster, windows of flame.

After Reading Tu Fu, I Go
Outside to the Dwarf Orchard

East of me, west of me, full summer.
How deeper than elsewhere the dusk is in your own yard.
Birds fly back and forth across the lawn
                                        looking for home
As night drifts up like a little boat.

Day after day, I become of less use to myself.
Like this mockingbird,
                        I flit from one thing to the next.
What do I have to look forward to at fifty-four?
Tomorrow is dark.
                    Day-after-tomorrow is darker still.

The sky dogs are whimpering.
Fireflies are dragging the hush of evening
                                        up from the damp grass.
Into the world's tumult, into the chaos of every day,
Go quietly, quietly.

Thinking of David Summers
at the Beginning of Winter

December, five days till Christmas,
      mercury red-lined
In the low twenties, glass throat
Holding the afternoon half-hindered
And out of luck.
     Goodbye to my last poem, "Autumn Thoughts."

Two electric wall heaters
      thermostat on and off,
Ice one-hearted and firm in the mouth of the downspout
Outside, snow stiff as a wedding dress
Carelessly left unkempt
     all week in another room.

Everything we desire is somewhere else,
       day too short,
Night too short, light snuffed and then relit,
Road salted and sanded down,
Sky rolling the white of its eye back
      into its head.

Reinvention is what we're after,
      Pliny's outline,
Living in history without living in the past
Is what the task is,
Quartering our desire,
     making what isn't as if it were.

Cicada

All morning I've walked about,
                                opening books and closing books,
Sitting in this chair and that chair.
Steady drip on the skylight,
                                steady hum of regret.
Who listens to anyone?
Across the room, bookcases,
                                across the street, summer trees.

Hear what the book says:
                                This earthly light
Is a seasoning, tempting and sweet and dangerous.
Resist the allurements of the eye.
Feet still caught in the toils of this world's beauty,
                                                                resist
The gratifications of the eye.

———————

Noon in the early September rain.
A cicada whines,
                    his voice
Starting to drown through the rainy world,
No ripple of wind,
                    no sound but his song of black wings,
No song but the song of his black wings.

Such emptiness at the heart,
                                such emptiness at the heart of being,

Fills us in ways we can't lay claim to,
Ways immense and without names,
                              husk burning like amber
On tree bark, cicada wind-bodied,
Leaves beginning to rustle now
                              in the dark tree of the self.

———————

If time is water, appearing and disappearing
In one heliotropic cycle,
                              this rain
That sluices as through an hourglass
Outside the window into the gutter and downspout,
Measures our nature
                              and moves the body to music.

The book says, however,
                              time is not body's movement
But memory of body's movement.
Time is not water but the memory of water:
We measure what isn't there.
We measure the silence.
                              We measure the emptiness.

Tennessee Line

Afternoon overcast the color of water
                      smoothed by clouds
That whiten where they enter the near end of the sky.
First day of my fifty-fifth year,
Last week of August limp as a frayed rope in the trees,
Yesterday's noise a yellow dust in my shirt pocket
Beneath the toothpick,
                 the .22 bullet and Amitone.

Sounds drift through the haze,
The shadowless orchard, peach leaves dull in the tall grass,
No wind, no bird shudder.
Green boat on the red Rivanna.
                  Rabbit suddenly in place
By the plum tree, then gone in three bounds.
Downshift of truck gears.

———————

In 1958, in Monterey, California,
I wrote a journal of over one hundred pages
About the Tennessee line,
About my imagined unhappiness,
                 and how the sun set like a coffin
Into the grey Pacific.
How common it all was.
             How uncommon I pictured myself.

Memento scrivi, skull-like and word-drunk,
                                one hundred fourteen pages
Of inarticulate self-pity
Looking at landscape and my moral place within it,
The slurry of words inexorable and dark,
The ethical high ground inexorable and dark
I droned from
                hoping for prescience and a shibboleth . . .

———————

I remember the word and forget the word
                                although the word
Hovers in flame around me.
Summer hovers in flame around me.
The overcast breaks like a bone above the Blue Ridge.
A loneliness west of solitude
Splinters into the landscape
                                uncomforting as Braille.

We *are* our final vocabulary,
                        and how we use it.
There is no secret contingency.
There's only the rearrangement, the redescription
Of little and mortal things.
There's only this single body, this tiny garment
Gathering the past against itself,
                                making it otherwise.

Looking Outside the Cabin Window, I Remember a Line by Li Po

The river winds through the wilderness,
Li Po said
               of another place and another time.
It does so here as well, sliding its cargo of dragon scales
To gutter under the snuff
               of marsh willow and tamarack.

Mid-morning, Montana high country,
Jack snipe poised on the scarred fence post,
Pond water stilled and smoothed out,
Swallows dog-fighting under the fast-moving storm clouds.

Expectantly empty, green as a pocket, the meadow waits
For the wind to rise and fill it,
               first with a dark hand
Then with the rain's loose silver
A second time and a third
               as the day doles out its hours.

Sunlight reloads and ricochets off the window glass.
Behind the cloud scuts,
               inside the blue aorta of the sky,
The River of Heaven flows
With its barge of stars,
               waiting for darkness and a place to shine.

We who would see beyond seeing
               see only language, that burning field.

TERRA COGNITA

Mid-winter Snowfall
in the Piazza Dante

Verona, late January . . .
                              Outside the caffè,
The snow, like papier-mâché, settles
Its strips all over Dante's bronze body, and holds fast.

Inside, a grappa
In one hand, a double espresso in the other,
I move through the room, slowly,
                              from chessboard to chessboard.

It's Tuesday, tournament night.
Dante's statue, beyond the window, grows larger and whiter
Under the floodlights
                    and serious Alpine snowfall.

In here I understand nothing,
                          not the chess, not the language,
Not even the narrow, pointed shoes the men all wear.
It's 1959. It's ten-thirty at night. I've been in the country for one week.

The nineteenth-century plush
                              on the chairs and loveseats
Resonates, purple and gold.
Three boards are in play in the front room, one in the bar.

My ignorance is immense,
                    as is my happiness.

Caught in the glow of all things golden
And white, I think, at twenty-three, my life has finally begun.

At a side table, under
The tulip-shaped lamps, a small group drinks to a wedding:
"*Tutti maschi*," the groom toasts,
                              and everyone lifts his full glass.

The huge snowflakes like soft squares
Alternately black and white in the flat light of the piazza,
I vamp in the plush and gold of the mirrors,
                              in love with the world.

That was thirty years ago.
I've learned a couple of things since then
                              not about chess
Or plush or all things golden and white.

Unlike a disease, whatever I've learned
Is not communicable.
                    A singular organism,
It does its work in the dark.

Anything that we think we've learned,
                              we've learned in the dark.
If there is one secret to this life, it is this life.
This life and its hand-me-downs,
                              bishop to pawn 4, void's gambit.

Sprung Narratives

What were we thinking of,
                              where were we trying to go,
My brother and I,
That March afternoon almost forty-five years ago,
Up U.S. 11W,
Snow falling, aged ten and eight,
                              so many miles from anyone we knew?

Past Armour Drug, the Civic Auditorium, Brooks Circle
And up the four-lane highway,
Past cornfield and sedgebrush field,
                              past the stone diner and Hillcrest,
Then up the mountain,
Five miles in the late snow,
                              unsure of our whereabouts.

Home, of course, parents abstract with dread,
Three months in a new town,
                              Second World War just over
Some six months before,
                              home to the only home we knew.
Or would know from that day on.
We'd missed the bus. We didn't know what else we should do.

Half-hallowed, half-hand-me-down,
                              our adolescence loomed
At walk's end, eager to gather us.

We let it.
And learned to dance with it, cumbersome, loath, in our arms.
And learned its numbers.
                    And learned its names.

How impossible now to reach it,
No matter how close we come
                    driving by in the car—
That childhood,
That landscape we pictured ourselves a no-cut part of
For good—
          each time we revisit it.

———————

Returned to the dwarf orchard,
                    Pilgrim,
Sit still and lengthen your lines,
Shorten your poems and listen to what the darkness says
With its mouthful of cold air.

Midnight, cloud-scatter and cloud-vanish,
                    sky black-chill and black-clear,
South wind through the March-bare trees,
House shadows and hedge shadows.
It's your life. Take it.
          Next month, next year, who knows where you will be.

———————

It's Saturday night,
                    summer of 1963,
The Teatro Farnese in Rome.

For 150 lire,
             it's Sordi and Gassman
In Mario Monicelli's *La Grande Guerra.*

Alberto Sordi and Vittorio Gassman, World War I
And the north Italian front.
                            Such unwilling heroes!
Sordi a Roman, Gassman a conscript from the Veneto,
Each speaking his dialect,
             each speaking, to my ears, as though in tongues.

But not to the *romanacci*
                       howling in recognition,
Sending each *stronzo*, each *fijo de na mignota*,
Back at the screen in an ecstasy
Of approval. Who *are* you, it asks?
                       Semmo l'anima de li mortacci tui . . .

Who knows what the story line
                            became, what happened to happen
At movie's end. What's brought back
Is not the occasion but its events,
                            the details
Surrounding it that nicked us.

The world is a language we never quite understand,
But think we catch the drift of.
                            Speaking in ignorance
And joy, we answer
What wasn't asked, by someone we don't know, in strange tongues,

Hoping to get the roll right—
Across the Tiber,
                    past Belli and Dante, off to supper
Scorching the kamikaze Fiats,
A *li mortacci tui, brutto zozzo, v'a fa'un culo* . . .

After it's over, after the last gaze has shut down,
Will I have become
The landscape I've looked at and walked through
Or the road that took me there
                    or the time it took to arrive?

How are we balanced out,
                    by measure, number and weight
As the Renaissance had it,
The idea of God with a compass or gold protractor in his hand?
Lovely to think so,
                    the landscape and journey as one . . .

Seventeen years in Laguna Beach—
Month after month the same weather,
                    year after year the same blue
Stretched like a tent-half above our heads.
Even the rain was predictable
When it rounded the Isthmus on Catalina
                    and curtained ashore.

Even the waves seemed laid back
And cool,
            tweaking the beaches with their tremulous sighs

Of smooth self-satisfaction,
Barely filling the tide pools,
                    languishing back and forth
Between moon-pull and earth-pull.

The walkway unwound along the cliffs
Overlooking all this,
                    and dipped to the pale shoreline
Like an Ace bandage. Down it I went
Each afternoon that I could,
Down to the burning sand,
                    down to the lid of the ocean's great blind eye.

Always the same ghost-figures
Haunting the boardwalk, the basketball courts and the beach.
Always the same shades
                    turning their flat, cocoa-buttered faces
Into the sun-glare,
Pasty, unchangeable faces,
                    unchangeable bodies impatient, unfulfilled.

I walked among them, booted, black-jacketed, peering
Unsurreptitiously into
                    whatever was recognizable.
I never knew anyone.
The sea with its one eye stared. I stared.
For seventeen years we both stared
                    as they turned like blank souls toward the sun.

——————

This text is a shadow text.
Under its images, under its darkened prerogatives,

Lie the lines of youth,
                    golden, and lipped in a white light.
They sleep as their shadows move

As though in a dream,
                    disconnected, unwished-upon.
And slightly distorted. And slightly out of control.
Their limbs gleam and their eyelids gleam,
                                        under whose soft skin
The little dances and paroxysms leap and turn.

———————

Spot, pivot and spin . . . Spot, pivot and spin . . .
                                        Esposito breaks
From the black-robed, black-cordovaned
Body of student priests
                    and feints down the wave-tongued sand
Like a fabulous bird where the tide sifts out and in.

His cassock billows and sighs
As he sings a show tune this morning at Ostia,
Rehearsing the steps and pirouettes
                              he had known by heart once
Last year in another life.

Behind him, like small fists,
                    the others open and close
Around the two German girls
Whose father has laid on and paid for
Their trip to the beach with American priests-to-be

Who drink at his *birreria* on Via della Croce.
September, still 1963.
Two months from now, Jerry Jacobson
Will burst through the door
Of my tiny apartment on Via del Babuino

And tell me that President Kennedy has been shot.
Two months.
But for now Esposito
Relives his turns and stage days,
The priests remember or reinvent,
Maria Luisa

And Astrid pretend
their charms will never dissolve or die back
In marriage and motherhood,
And I, the teacher of noun and verb
in a language they can't quite understand,
Hum with Esposito and covet their golden hair.

————————

Something surrounds us we can't exemplify, something
Mindless and motherless,
dark as diction and twice told.
We hear it at night.
Flake by flake,
we taste it like tinfoil between our teeth.

Under the little runnels of snow,
under the mist
settling like moonlight

Over the orchard,
                    under the grasses and black leaves,
In its hush, in its sky width, it takes our breath away.

————————

How small it is, and remote,
                    like a photograph from a friend's album
Of the house he lived in as a child.
Or our house seen from next door
Through the bathroom window,
                              a curtain pushed to one side.
How barren the porch looks, how forlorn the rosebushes.

Inside the front room, there are different lights in different places.
Different cars block the driveway.
Where has the tree gone
                    that feathered the summer air with music?
Where is the white throat
That settled the dark, and that darkness settled itself inside?

The valley has been filled in
                    with abandoned structures.
New roads that have been bypassed
By newer roads
                    glint in the late sun and disappear.
As the twilight sinks in
Across the landscape,
                    lights come on like the lights next door . . .

Seeing the past so
                    diminishes it and us too,
Both of us crowding the ghost ramp

And path along the strawberry patch and peanut field,
Down through the hemlocks and apple trees
Behind the house,
                    into the black hole of history.

What's left?
            A used leaf shredder, empty begonia pots,
Some memory like a dot
Of light retreating, smaller and sharper with each glance,
Nobody left to remember it
But us,
        half hidden behind a bathroom window curtain? I guess so.

Lines on Seeing a Photograph for the First Time in Thirty Years

It's 1959,
        black horn-rims and duffle coats,
Black stockings.
Lake Garda, Punto San Vigilio.
           Deep winter,
Waves like shark fins beyond the archway.
I have my motif
        but haven't broken it down yet.
Lakescape and memory. Waterscald.

San Vigilio crooks like a little finger into the lake
Just above Garda.
Oliveshine, leaf click.
        Wind from Salò, clouds from Salò,
Shadows from west to east on the lake's back and land's back,
West to east, the water reeds
Feathery half-brown,
        stiff in the wavelap's nudge and spray.

Ingrid and Charles, Italianate
        on the stone steps.
Behind their fixed stares,
Nothing is turning its palms up, nothing is starting to roll
Out of their future like a charred wheel.
Only the water moves behind their backs,
        constant and fin-like,
Begging the question, begging the scene.

There's no indication of time's brush
And time's ink that will transfigure them
Into the lakescape's lockbox
                              of sepia halftones,
Half lost and half forgotten.
And no indication of what looms
Behind the photographer's back,
                              at ease and pulling its ghost gloves on.

Memories never lie still.
                              They circle the landscape
Like hawks on the wind,
Turning and widening, their centers cut loose and disappearing,
Tiny cracks in the mind's sky,
Sheenlines, afterglint.
The world is small and blue.
                              These are the lights we look for.

BROKEN ENGLISH

Broken English

Spring like smoke in the fruit trees,
Ambulance siren falling away
                              through the thick grass.
I gaze at the sky and cut lines from my long poem.

————————

What matters we only tell ourselves.

Without the adjective there is no evil or good.

All speech pulls toward privacy
                              and the zones of the infinite.

Better to say what you mean than to mean what you say.

Without a syntax, there is no immortality.

————————

Truth's an indefinite article.
When we live, we live for the last time,
                              as Akhmatova says,
One *the* in a world of *a*.

Maple on the Hill

October again. Faint pheasant tail
Slips through and ruffles the maple tree.
                 A few feathers
Leaf down to cuckold the grass.
Power lines shine, cars shine.
             Season of glass-glint and edge,

Abracadabra of sunlight,
             cut and spin.
The day saws itself in half.
Northwest wind has something up its sleeve.
At the horned heart of the labyrinth,
             the unsayable has its say.

———————

Don't forget me, little darling, when they've laid me down to die.
Just one little wish, darling, that I pray.
As you linger there in sadness you are thinking of the past,
Let your teardrops kiss the flowers on my grave.

———————

The mirror of history swallows its images:
It never repeats itself
             in us, its distorted children.
Each life, as Plutarch tells us,
Contains many lives,
             some recognizable, some not.

History's just another story.
In the City of the Dead, no one
                    stands up and says, *Here I am, I'm your boy.*
Discontinuous, discrete,
The hunter, history's dog, will sniff us,
                                        sure as hell . . .

Black and Blue

Rain is a dangerous thing.
                    It shrinks and squats the years
We've come to count on.
With its good eye and its bad eye,
                    it settles them back to size.

———————

Like deer in a leafy light,
                    window and looking glass,
Yesterdays flash and reflect,
Ready to bolt, ready to empty out.
                    Horizon them black and blue.

———————

White water like white flags,
                    streamers, little prayer beacons,
Back in the North Fork of Basin Creek,
Beckons our memory.
                    But never the same flag twice.

———————

Hawk planes over marsh grass,
                    low over marsh grass and meadow weed.
Hawk pivots, folds and unfolds, drops and rises like string.
Unseen, under the dun mat and wattle runs,
                    something is always there.

———————

The road to Damascus runs through
                              the veins in the lilac's leaf.
Ararat pokes through the daisy's eye.
Crows at the salt block
            pick their way through the back streets of Carthage.

———————

Sunglasses. Hands on his hips
                              like Montgomery Clift. Levis.
Cistercian courtyard. Saint Something-or-other. Weeds.
A chain saw clears its throat.
                  Like blue balloons, we disappear in the sky.

———————

The dead have lives of their own.
                  They glide, like round, radiant pearls of light,
Under our feet, stopping, from time to time, to handcup an ear.
Listen, they think, on the room roof,
                              faint footfalls of the unborn.

———————

Beautiful stars of the Bear,
                  Dipper
Unchanged of all the waters that blessed my youth, sprinkle
Me now,
            cross and burn.

———————

The wind shifts, the landscape turns in its sleep.
                              Seasons slough and rinse.
Like trees, we fall in the dark forest and make no sound.
The deer never raise their heads.
            The voles never miss a step through the mystical sloughgrass.

Two boys in sateen bathing suits.

                             Lunch box. Stringer of sunfish.

Father-shadow. Half father-shadow

Draining out of the photograph.

                             Summer again. It's summer.

Our lives are an emptiness

                        at rest in the present.

Dark cloud, bright cloud, sunlight, rain.

Great wind keeps carrying us

                      where we don't want, where we don't know.

Chickamauga

Dove-twirl in the tall grass.
                         End-of-summer glaze next door
On the gloves and split ends of the conked magnolia tree.
Work sounds: truck back-up-beep, wood tin-hammer, cicada, fire
    horn.

History handles our past like spoiled fruit.
Mid-morning, late-century light
                         calicoed under the peach trees.
Fingers us here. Fingers us here and here.

The poem is a code with no message:
The point of the mask is not the mask but the face underneath,
Absolute, incommunicado,
                         unhoused and peregrine.

The gill net of history will pluck us soon enough
From the cold waters of self-contentment we drift in
One by one
                         into its suffocating light and air.

Structure becomes an element of belief, syntax
And grammar a catechist,
Their words what the beads say,
                         words thumbed to our discontent.

ROSA MISTICA

Still Life on a Matchbox Lid

The heart is colder than the eye is.
The watchers, the holy ones,
                        know this, no shortcut to the sky.
A single dog hair can split the wind.

If you want great tranquillity,
                        it's hard work and a long walk.
Don't brood on the past.
The word is without appendages,
                        no message, no name.

Blaise Pascal Lip-syncs the Void

It's not good to be complete.
It's not good to be concupiscent,
                    caught as we are
Between a the and a the,
Neither of which we know and neither of which knows us.
It's not good to be sewn shut.

There's change and succession in all things, Pascal contends,
But inconstancy, boredom and anxiety condition our days.
Neither will wash for him, though,
                        since nature is corrupt.
That's why we love it.
                That's why we take it, unwinnowed,
Willingly into our hearts.

December. 4 p.m.
                Chardonnay-colored light-slant
Lug weight in the boned trees.
                        Squirrel dead on the Tarmac.
Boom-boxing Big Foot pickup trucks
Hustle down Locust,
            light pomegranate pink grapefruit then blood.
We take it into our hearts.

Winter-Worship

Mother of Darkness, Our Lady,
Suffer our supplications,
                    our hurts come unto you.
Hear us from absence your dwelling place,
Whose ear we plead for.
                    End us our outstay.

Where darkness is light, what can the dark be,
                              whose eye is single,
Whose body is filled with splendor
In winter,
          inside the snowflake, inside the crystal of ice
Hung like Jerusalem from the tree.

January, rain-wind and sleet-wind,
Snow pimpled and pock-marked,
                         half slush-hearted, half brocade,
Under your noon-dimmed day watch,
Whose alcove we harbor in,
                    whose waters are beaded and cold.

A journey's a fragment of Hell,
                         one inch or a thousand miles.
Darken our disbelief, dog our steps.
Inset our eyesight,
Radiance, loom and sting,
                    whose ashes rise from the flames.

The Silent Generation

Afternoons in the backyard, our lives like photographs
Yellowing elsewhere,
                     in somebody else's album,
In secret, January south winds
Ungathering easily through the black limbs of the fruit trees.

What was it we never had to say?
                           Who can remember now—
Something about the world's wrongs,
Something about the way we shuddered them off like rain
In an open field,
                  convinced that lightning would not strike.

We're arm in arm with regret, now left foot, now right foot.
We give the devil his due.
We walk up and down in the earth,
                       we take our flesh in our teeth.
When we die, we die. The wind blows away our footprints.

An Ordinary Afternoon
in Charlottesville

Under the peach trees, the ideograms the leaves throw
Over the sun-prepped grass read
Purgatio, illuminatio, contemplatio,
Words caught in a sweet light endurable,
                              unlike the one they lead to,
Whose sight we're foundered and fallowed by.

Meanwhile, the afternoon
                    fidgets about its business,
Unconcerned with such immolations,
Sprinkle of holy grit from the sun's wheel,
                              birds combustible
In the thin leaves incendiary—
Fire, we think, marvellous fire, everything starts in fire.

Or so they say. We like to think so
Ourselves, feeling the cold
                    glacier into the blood stream
A bit more each year,
Tasting the iron disk on our tongues,
Watching the birds oblivious,
                    hearing their wise chant, *hold still, hold still* . . .

Tom Strand and the Angel of Death

What does the Angel of Death look like,
                                   my friend's son asked.
White, with a pointed head and an orange skirt, my friend replied.
Down to the stem she swirls on,   ·
I thought to myself, for no reason,
                              seeing her rise from gorse and broom
Like a column of crystal.

Or like the sun, I should have thought,
                                   spinning above our heads,
Centrifugal force of all we do.
This evening, under Mount Caribou, I remember her skirt and stem
In the black meadow grass,
                              eyes shaded against the dark,
Bone of her bone and flesh of her flesh:

Oil-rag American sky,
August night wind rummaging back and forth in the pines,
Stars falling beyond the Yukon—
                              chrome-vanishing stars,
Insistent inside the heart's Arctic—
Unbroken code,
                   this life that is handed us, this this . . .

Mondo Angelico

Fish never sleep.
                     Aquatic angels,
They drift in the deep ether of all their rectitude,
Half dark, half flicker of light
At the eye's edge,
                     their shadows shadows of shadows—

Under the blue spruce,
Under the skunkweed and onion head,
Under the stump,
                     the aspergillum of the dew-rose,
They signal and disappear.

Like lost thoughts,
                     they wouldn't remember us if they could,
Hovering just out of touch,
Their bodies liminal, their sights sealed.
Always they disregard us
                     with a dull disregard.

Mondo Henbane

The journey ends between the black spiders and the white spiders,
As Blake reminds us.
                              For now,
However, pain is the one thing that fails to actualize
Where the green-backed tree swallows dip
                                        and the wood ducks glide

Over the lodgepole's soft slash.
Little islands of lime-green pine scum
Float on the pot-pond water.
                              Load-heavy bumblebees
Lower themselves to the sun-swollen lupine and paintbrush throats.

In the front yard, a half mile away,
                              one robin stretches his neck out,
Head cocked to the ground,
Hearing the worm's hum or the worm's heart.
Or hearing the spiders fly,
                    on their fiery tracks, through the smoke-choked sky.

Miles Davis and Elizabeth Bishop
Fake the Break

Those two dark syllables, *begin*,
                              offer no sustenance,
Nor does this pale squish of September sunlight unwound
Across the crabgrass.

The silence is cold, like an instrument in the hand
Which cannot be set aside,
Unlike our suffering, so easy, so difficult.

Still, the warmth on our skin is nice,
                              and the neighbor's pears,
Late pears, dangle like golden hourglasses above our heads.

"It's just description," she said,
                              "they're all just description."
Meaning her poems . . . Mine, too,
The walleye of morning's glare
                              lancing the landscape,
The dogwood berries as red as cinnamon drops in the trees,
Sunday, the twenty-ninth of September, 1991.

From the top . . . Beginning in ignorance, we stick to the melody—
Knowledge, however, is elsewhere,
                              a tune we've yet to turn to,
Its syllables scrubbed in light, its vestibules empty.

Peccatology

As Kafka has told us,
                              sin always comes openly:
It walks on its roots and doesn't have to be torn out.

How easily it absolves itself in the senses,
However, in Indian summer,
                              the hedge ivy's star-feet
Treading the dead spruce and hemlock spurs,
The last leaves like live coals
                              banked in the far corners of the yard,
The locust pods in Arabic letters, right to left.

How small a thing it becomes, nerve-sprung
And half electric,
                              deracinated, full of joy.

East of the Blue Ridge,
Our Tombs Are in the Dove's Throat

Late Sunday in Charlottesville.
We cross our arms like effigies, look up at the sky
And wait for a sign of salvation—
                            as Lorca has taught us to say,
Two and two never make four down here,
They always make two and two.

Five crows roust a yellow-tailed hawk from the hemlock tree next door,
Black blood spots dipping and blown
Across the relentless leeching
                        the sun pales out of the blue.

We'd like to fly away ourselves, pushed
Or pulled, into or out of our own bodies,
                            into or out of the sky's mouth.
We'd like to disappear into a windfall of light.

But the numbers don't add up.
Besides, a piece of jar glass
                        burns like a star at the street's edge,
The elbows and knuckled limb joints of winter trees,
Shellacked by the sunset, flash and fuse,
Windows blaze
            and the earthly splendor roots our names to the ground.

"Not everyone can see the truth, but he can be it"

Sunday. It's always Sunday.
                              Rifts and seams of dark birds
Right-flank and wheel across a darker December sky
Southwest and so wide.

Winter solstice again,
                              burnt end of a narrow road.
The lawn chairs gutter and glare in their white solitude.

How short the days are.

How imperceptibly we become ourselves—
                              like solstice-diminishing light
Devolving to one appointed spot,
We substitute and redress
In predetermined degrees we've neither a heart nor hand in.

How slowly the streetlights come on.
                              How shrill the birds are.

Take off your traveling clothes and
                              lay down your luggage,
Pilgrim, shed your nakedness.
Only the fire is absorbed by the Holy of Holies.
                              Let it shine.

As Our Bodies Rise,
Our Names Turn into Light

The sky unrolls like a rug,
                                unwelcoming, gun-grey,
Over the Blue Ridge.
Mothers are calling their children in,
                          mellifluous syllables, floating sounds.
The traffic shimmies and settles back.

The doctor has filled his truck with leaves
Next door, and a pair of logs.
                             Salt stones litter the street.
The snow falls and the wind drops.
How strange to have a name, any name, on this poor earth.

January hunkers down,
                         the icicle deep in her throat—
The days become longer, the nights ground bitter and cold,
Single grain by single grain
Everything flows toward structure,
                              last ache in the ache for God.

Absence Inside an Absence

We live in the world of the voice,

                          not in the world of the word,

According to John the Solitary—
Our lives are language, our desires are apophatic,
The bush in flame is the bush in flame,
Imageless heart, imageless absence between the hearts.

And if we cry out,

                   if once we utter our natural sounds,

Even the angels will hide their heads
Under their blue wings,

                       it's also said.

So better forget that, better forget the darkness above the tongue,
Its shorting of words, its mad silence and lack of breath.

Besides, there's another spin,
The flame and counterflame by which we come to stillness
Playing over our faces,

                   over the rose cane and the missing rose,

Over the dreary schooners of snow
Pulling their nets in across the yard,

                       over their waters brought to joy.

Still, the idea of absence inside an absence
Completing a presence is dynamite,

                    the showings foretold
Unseeable through the earthly eye,
We say to ourselves,
The earth in our cracked hands,
             the earth dark syllables in our mouths.

Still Life with Spring
and Time to Burn

Warm day, early March. The buds preen, busting their shirtwaists
All over the plum trees. Blue moan of the mourning dove.
It's that time again,
                                    time of relief, time of sorrow
The earth is afflicted by.
We feel it ourselves, a bright uncertainty of what's to come

Swelling our own skins with sweet renewal, a kind of disease
That holds our affections dear
                                    and asks us to love it.
And so we do, supposing
That time and affection is all we need answer to.
But we guess wrong:

Time will append us like suit coats left out overnight
On a deck chair, loose change dead weight in the right pocket,
Silk handkerchief limp with dew,
                                    sleeves in a slow dance with the wind.
And love will kill us—
Love, and the winds from under the earth
                                    that grind us to grain-out.

Morandi II

Brushstroke and buringouge, cups
                                    huddled together, black and white,
Still life and landscape, perspective and architecture,
Giorgio Morandi stayed home
And kept his distance and measure. And kept his silence.
No word for anything but his work.

Example: yellow and tan,
                        rectangle, circle, square.
Example: cylinder, black and brown,
Table-line like a horizon one might approach from.
Example: angle and plane,
Scratches like an abyss,
                        a Mondrian-absence one might descend to.

Corners of buildings, bottles, hillsides, shade trees and fields,
Color and form, light and space,
                                the losses we get strange gain from.

With Simic and Marinetti
at the Giubbe Rosse

Where Dino Campana once tried to sell his sad poems
Among the tables,
Where Montale settled into his silence and hid,
Disguised as himself for twenty years,
The ghosts of Papini and Prezzolini sit tight
With Carlo Emilio Gadda

somewhere behind our backs.

Let's murder the moonlight, let's go down
On all fours and mewl like the animals and make it mean what it
means.
Not even a stir.
Not even a breath across the plates of *gnocchi* and roast veal.
Like everything else in Florence, that's part of the past,
The wind working away away kneading the sea so muscles . . .

Those who don't remember the Futurists are condemned to repeat
them.
We order a grappa. We order a mineral water.
Little by little, the lucid, warm smile of the moon
Overflowed from the torn clouds.

Some ran.
A cry was heard in the solitude of the high plains.
Simic e Wright sulla traccia. La luna ammazzata.

To the Egyptian Mummy in
the Etruscan Museum at Cortona

Wrapped like a sprained ankle from head to toe,
>   locked in glass
In an inconceivable country,
Spun on the sprung reflections caught in a stranger's eye
Year after year,
>   you would not imagine yourself if you could,
Peninsulaed as you are, and rare.

Outside the window, sun rains on the Middle Ages.
An upupa pecks in the tall grass.
Under the stone walls and stone towers,
>   the hillside unravels its tapestry,
A picnic in spring's green fire: one man's asleep and a young girl
Claps time for her brother who hand-dances with his dog.

One half-expects, say, Guidoriccio da Fogliano
In full regalia,
Or Maiatesta, at least, at large from the Marches,
To climb the gut-twisted road through the quicksilver glint and tufa
>   stone
Toward the south gate and you,
>   pale messenger from the wordless world . . .

Leonardo, Vasari says,
>   would purchase the caged, white doves
As he walked through the market sprawl of San Lorenzo

In order to set them free. I'll do
The same thing for you, unlatching this landscape, the vine rows and
    olive trees,
Till its wingspread shrinks to a radiance.
                        Look. Already it's getting smaller.

With Eddie and Nancy in Arezzo
at the Caffè Grande

Piero in wraps, the True Cross *sotto restauro*,
Piazza desolate edge
Where sunlight breaks it,
                            desolate edge
Where sunlight pries it apart.
A child kicks a soccer ball. Another heads it back.

The Fleeting World, Po Chü-i says, short-hops a long dream,
No matter if one is young or old—
The pain of what is present never comes to an end,
Lightline moving inexorably
West to east across the stones,
                            cutting the children first, then cutting us.

Under the archways, back and forth among the tables,
The blind ticket seller taps and slides.
Lotteria di Foligno, Lotteria di Foligno,
                            he intones,
Saturday, mid-May, cloud bolls high cotton in the Tuscan sky.
One life is all we're entitled to, but it's enough.

There Is No Shelter

Each evening, the sins of the whole world collect here like a dew.
In the morning, little galaxies, they flash out
And flame,
           their charred, invisible residue etching

The edges our lives take and the course of things, filling
The shadows in,
           an aftertrace, through the discards of the broken world,
Like the long, slow burn of a struck match.

CHINA STARS

Watching the Equinox Arrive
in Charlottesville, September 1992

2:23 p.m.
        The season glides to a click.
Nobody says a word
From where I sit, shadows dark flags from nothing's country,
Birds in the deep sky, then not,
Cricket caught in the outback between a grass spear and a leaf.
The quince bush
Is losing its leaves in the fall's early chemotherapy,
And stick-stemmed spikes of the lemon tree
Spink in the sun.
Autumnal outtakes, autumnal stills . . .

Mockingbird, sing me a song.
Back here, where the windfall apples rot to the bee's joy,
Where the peach sheaths and pear sheaths piebald and brindle,
Where each year the orchard unlearns
                      everything it's been taught,
The weekend's rainfall
Pools its untroubled waters,
Doves putter about in the still-green limbs of the trees,
Ants inch up the cinder blocks and lawn spiders swing from the vines.
You've got to learn to unlearn things, the season repeats.
For every change there's a form.

Open your mouth, you are lost, close your mouth, you are lost,
So the Buddhists say.
        They also say,

Live in the world unattached to the dust of the world.
Not so easy to do when the thin, monotonous tick of the universe
Painfully pries our lips apart,
                              and dirties our tongues
With soiled, incessant music.
Not so easy to do when the right front tire blows out,
Or the phone rings at 3 a.m.
                         and the ghost-voice says, "It's 911, please hold."
They say, enter the blackness, the form of forms. They say,
No matter how we see ourselves, sleeping and dreaming see us as light.

Still, there's another story,
                          that what's inside us is what's outside us:
That what we see outside ourselves we'll soon see inside ourselves.
It's visible, and is our garment.
Better, perhaps, to wear that.
Better to live as though we already lived the afterlife,
Unattached to our cape of starred flesh.
But Jesus said,
                Lift up the stone and you will find me,
Break open a piece of wood, I'm there.
It's hard to argue with that,
Hard to imagine a paradise beyond what the hand breaks.

———————

For every force there's a change.
Mouthful of silence, mouthful of air,
                                    sing me your tune.
The wind leaves nothing alone.
How many times can summer turn to fall in one life?
Well you might ask, my old friend,
Wind-rider, wind-spirit, seeking my blood out,

                              humming my name.
Hard work, this business of solitude.
Hard work and no gain,
Mouthful of silence, mouthful of air.
Everything's more than it seems back here. Everything's less.

Like migrating birds, our own lives drift away from us.
How small they become in the blank sky, how colorful,
On their way to wherever they please.
We keep our eyes on the ground,
                              on the wasp and pinch bug,
As the years grind by and the seasons churn, north and south.
We keep our eyes on the dirt.
Under the limp fins of the lemon tree, we inhabit our absence.
Crows cross-hatch and settle in,
                              red birds and dust sparrows
Spindle and dart through the undergrowth.
We don't move. We watch, but we don't move.

Waiting for Tu Fu

Snip, snip goes wind through the autumn trees.
I move my bed to the battlefront,
      dead leaves like a blanket of moth bodies
Up to the necks of the cold grasses.
It crunches like pecan shells underfoot.
It crinks my back where I lie
      gazing into the beaten artifice
Of gold leaf and sky.

How vast the clouds are, how vast as they troll and pass by.
Splendid and once-removed, like lives, they never come back.
Does anyone think of them?
Everything's golden from where I lie.
      Even the void
Beyond the void the clouds cross.
Even the knowledge that everything's fire,
      and nothing ever comes back.

All that was yesterday, or last week,
Or somebody else's line of talk.
      Words rise like mist from my body,
Prayer-smoke, a snowy comfort.
The Greek-thin hammered gold artifacts
      and glazed inlay
Of landscape and sky
Accept it as incense, for they are used to such things.

What have you done with your life,
                        you've asked me, as you've asked yourself,
What has it come to,
Carrying us like a barge toward the century's end
And sheer drop-off into millennial history?
I remember an organ chord one Sunday in North Carolina.
I remember the smell of white pines,
                        Vitalis and lye soap.

O we were pure and holy in those days,
The August sunlight candescing our short-sleeved shirt fronts,
The music making us otherwise.
O we were abstract and true.
How could we know that grace would fall from us like shed skin,
That reality, our piebald dog, would hunt us down?

The seasons reshuffle and set me.
Cattle as large as clouds
                        lumber across my mind's sky
And children rise in the wind
Like angels over the lake, sad cataracted eye—

I remember cutting its surface once in a green canoe,
Eye that saw everything, that now sees nothing at all . . .

Where is my life going in these isolate outlands,
You questioned once in a verse.
I ask the same thing,
                        wreckage of broken clouds too far to count,

The landscape, like God, a circle whose center is everywhere
And circumference nowhere,
Dead end of autumn, everything caught between stone-drift and stone.

Black winter bird flocks side-wheel
From tree lung to grief-empty tree lung,
                                    lawn furniture
Imprints, unsat in. It's late.
Darkness, black phosphorus, smokes forth in the peaches and white
    pines.
The pile driver footing the new bridge
Cuts off, the bird flocks cough up and out.

I've read *Reflections in Autumn*,
        I've been through the Three Gorges, I've done Chengdu . . .
Much easier here to find you out,
A landscape yourself by now,
Canebrake and waterbrake, inviolable in the memory.
Immortals, you once said, set forth again in their boats.
White hair, white hair. Drift away.

IMAGINARY ENDINGS

Paesaggio Notturno

Full moon, the eighth of March; clouds
Cull and disperse; dog's bark, moon
Tracking stage left to stage right;
Maple ganglia, Munch sky.

Small night that pulls me inside,
Fingerless, fatherless; night
Crystalline, sleep-shaped and sharp,
The bulb tufts odd teeth; nightmouth.

All things are found in all things,
Wind in the peach trees, time's dust:
It's in light that light exists.
All flesh, at last, comes to you.

Still Life with Stick and Word

April is over. May moon.
How many more for my regard,

                hundreds, a handful?
Better not trouble the dark water due north of north.
Better to concentrate on something close, something small.
This stick, for instance. This word.

Next week. Back in the same chair.
And here's the stick

             right where I dropped it, deep in the grass.
Maple, most likely, fuzz-barked and twice-broken, spore-pocked
With white spots, star charts to ford the river of heaven.
Warm wood. Warm wind from the clouds.

Inside now. The word is *white*.
It covers my tongue like paint—

                   I say it and light forms,
Bottles arise, emptiness opens its corridors
Into the entrances and endless things that form bears.
White, great eviscerator.

Out into absence. Night chair.
Rose constellations rise

                up from the shed and sad trees,
White yips in the dog dark that mirror the overburn.
A slide of houselight escapes through the kitchen window.
How unlike it is. How like.

Summer Storm

As Mondrian knew,
Art is the image of an image of an image,
More vacant, more transparent
With each repeat and slough:
                              one skin, two skins, it comes clear,
An old idea not that old.

Two rectangles, red and grey, from 1935,
Distant thunder like distant thunder—
Howitzer shells, large
                      dropoffs into drumbeat and roll.
And there's that maple again,
Head like an African Ice Age queen, full-leafed and lipped.

Behind her, like clear weather,
Mondrian's window gives out
                           onto ontology,
A dab of red, a dab of grey, white interstices.
You can't see the same thing twice,
As Mondrian knew.

Looking West from Laguna Beach
at Night

I've always liked the view from my mother-in-law's house at night,
Oil rigs off Long Beach
Like floating lanterns out in the smog-dark Pacific,
Stars in the eucalyptus,
Lights of airplanes arriving from Asia, and town lights
Littered like broken glass around the bay and back up the hill.

In summer, dance music is borne up
On the sea winds from the hotel's beach deck far below,
"Twist and Shout," or "Begin the Beguine."
It's nice to think that somewhere someone is having a good time,
And pleasant to picture them down there
Turned out, tipsy and flushed, in their white shorts and their turquoise
    shirts.

Later, I like to sit and look up
At the mythic history of Western civilization,
Pinpricked and clued through the zodiac.
I'd like to be able to name them, say what's what and how who got
    where,
Curry the physics of metamorphosis and its endgame,
But I've spent my life knowing nothing.

Looking Again at What I Looked At
for Seventeen Years

Quick pink; Soutine meat-streaks in the west,
Ocean grey drop cloth underfoot;
                              peroxided gums—
Memory's like that, mixed metaphors, time's drone and gouache
Hovering near the horizon, black
Instinct filling the edges in, resplendent with holes.

We have it for text and narrative—
                              nothing is new,
Remembrance, both nerve-net and nerve-spring,
The connection of everything with everything else
(Like absences the sea fills),
Constructs us and deconstructs us, world's breath, world's body.

Down there, for instance, just past the security lights
The hotel fans, wave-hollows build and dispense, surf sighs
And the unseen undertow
Sucks it away to where it's unreachable for good
Until it all comes back . . .
                              It's like that.

Looking Across Laguna Canyon at Dusk, West-by-Northwest

I love the way the evening sun goes down,
       orange brass-plaque, life's loss-logo,
Behind the Laguna hills and bare night-wisps of fog.
I love the way the hills empurple and sky goes nectarine,
The way the lights appear like little electric fig seeds, the wet west
Burnishing over into the indeterminate colors of the divine.

Like others, I want to pour myself into the veins of the invisible
at times like this,
      becoming all that's liquid and moist.
Like Dionysus, I'd enter the atmosphere, spread and abandon—
They'd have to look for me elsewhere then,
Trickle of light extinguished in the Pacific, dark sluice, dark sluice
  line.

Venexia I

Too much at first, too lavish—full moon
Jackhammering light-splints along the canal, gondola beaks
Blading the half-dark;
Moon-spar; backwash backlit with moon-spark . . .

Next morning, all's otherwise
With a slow, chill rainfall like ragweed
                               electric against the launch lights,
Then grim-grained, then grey.
This is the water-watch landscape, the auto-da-fé.

Such small atrocities these days between the columns,
Such pale seductions and ravishments.
Boats slosh on the crushed canal, gulls hunch down, the weather rubs
    us away.
From here it's a long walk home.

Listen, Venice is death by drowning, everyone knows,
City of masks and minor frightfulness, October city
Twice sunk in its own sad skin.
How silently the lagoon
                               covers our footsteps, how quickly.

Along the Zattere, the liners drift huge as clouds.
We husband our imperfections, our changes of tune.
When water comes for us, we take it into our arms—
What's left's affection, and that's our sin.

Venexia II

Acqua alta, high water,
                   sea gull anchored like Rimbaud's boat
Among the detritus, stuffed plastic food sacks bobbing like corks
Under Our Lady's stone-stern gaze,
                        Venezia, Serenissima . . .
Tide-slosh nibbles our shoe tops, then stumbles them under.

These are the dark waters, dark music
That scours us, that empties us out
                       only to fill us back by inches
With sweet, invisible plentitude,
Notes of astonishment, black notes to leave our lives by.

The Angel of Death, with her golden horn and her golden robe,
Rocks on the gondola's prow,
                     rain-dazzled, lashed at ease.
Under the rainfall's doom date,
She shines in her maritime solitude, she slides in splendor.

Outside the window, Rio San Polo churns and squalls.
The *traghetto*'s light
Burns like a homing Cathar soul
                     over the slack tide
Descending the greened Salute's steps.

This is the terminate hour, its bell
Tumbling out of Santa Maria Gloriosa dei Frari,
Last link in the chain of Speculation,
                                        pulling us under.
Water is what it comes from, water is where it goes.

Yard Work

I think that someone will remember us in another time,
Sappho once said—more or less—
Her words caught
Between the tongue's tip and the first edge of the invisible.

I hope so, myself now caught
Between the edge of the landscape and the absolute,
Which is the same place, and the same sound,
That she made.

Meanwhile, let's stick to business.
Everything else does, the landscape, the absolute, the invisible.
My job is yard work—
I take this inchworm, for instance, and move it from here to there.

NOTES

Aftermath

Contingency, Irony and Solidarity, Richard Rorty (Cambridge University Press, 1989).

Three Hundred Poems of the T'ang Dynasty, translator(s) anonymous (Hong Kong, undated).

Confessions, Saint Augustine (Penguin Books, 1961).

"Pliny's outline"—Pliny said the invention of painting occurred when a Corinthian maiden drew the outline of her lover after he went away to war, so she could remember what he looked like.

One Hundred Poems from the Chinese, Kenneth Rexroth (New Directions, 1956).

Broken English

Real Presences, George Steiner (University of Chicago Press, 1989).

Rosa Mistica

Pensées, Blaise Pascal, translated by A. J. Krailsheimer (Penguin Books, 1966).

The Songlines, Bruce Chatwin (Viking Penguin, 1988).

"The Man on the Dump," in *Collected Poems*, Wallace Stevens (Alfred A. Knopf, 1965).

The Blue Octavo Notebooks, Franz Kafka (Exact Change Press, 1990).

Collected Poems: Federico García Lorca, ed. Christopher Maurer (Farrar, Straus & Giroux, 1991).

"The Apophatic Image: The Poetics of Effacement in Julian of Norwich," Vincent Gillespie and Maggie Ross, in *The Medieval Mystical Tradition in England* (unpublished).

The Giubbe Rosse is a *caffè* in Florence, Italy.

China Stars

The Selected Poems of Tu Fu, translated by David Hinton (New Directions, 1989).
Poems of Paul Celan, translated by Michael Hamburger (Persea Books, 1988).

Imaginary Endings

Natura Morta, Giorgio Morandi, c. 1957, The University of Iowa Museum of Art.
"Full Feeling IV," Tu Fu, *Bright Moon, Perching Bird*, Seaton and Cryer translators (Wesleyan University Press, 1987).
Composition in Gray and Red, 1935, Piet Mondrian, The Art Institute of Chicago.
The Marriage of Cadmus and Harmony, Roberto Calasso, translated by Tim Parks (Alfred A. Knopf, 1993).